A Dash of Science

Liz Ray

Contents

Rigby
A Harcourt Achieve Imprint

www.Rigby.com
1-800-531-5015

Think about what you've eaten today. Maybe you had scrambled eggs and buttered toast for breakfast. Or maybe you had a bowl of cereal with a side of fruit. Most people think about the way food tastes but often they don't realize that cooking food can be like a scientific experiment.

This book will help you uncover some scientific secrets that are hiding in your refrigerator! You'll perform experiments and cook tasty snacks at the same time! No doubt you'll be amazed by the way different foods react to each other in this fun-filled book.

Common Cooking Abbreviations

tsp. = teaspoon

Tbs. = tablespoon

c. = cup

pt. = pint

qt. = quart

F = Fahrenheit

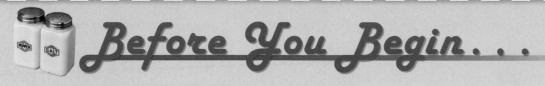

Before You Begin. . .

Before you begin your scientific experiments, it is important that you understand and follow certain safety precautions. By taking the necessary precautions, you're helping ensure that the outcome of each experiment will be successful . . . as well as tasty.

Safety Precautions

◆ Read each recipe completely before beginning.

◆ Gather the necessary equipment and ingredients ahead of time.

◆ Ask an adult for help.

◆ Use a potholder when handling pots and pans that have been heated. Remember, the handle can get hot too.

◆ Make sure that all pot and pan handles are positioned toward the back of the stove.

◆ Be careful not to overheat the ingredients. Hot oils and liquids that become too hot may splatter.

◆ Use extreme caution when a recipe or experiment calls for a knife, stove, or oven. Always ask an adult to help with these tasks.

◆ Be sure to keep your hands and fingers away from the blade when slicing food. Be sure to slice the food away from your body.

◆ Clean all utensils and equipment with soap and warm water after you've completed each recipe.

By staying organized, you're ensuring that your work area is safe.

That's Sick!

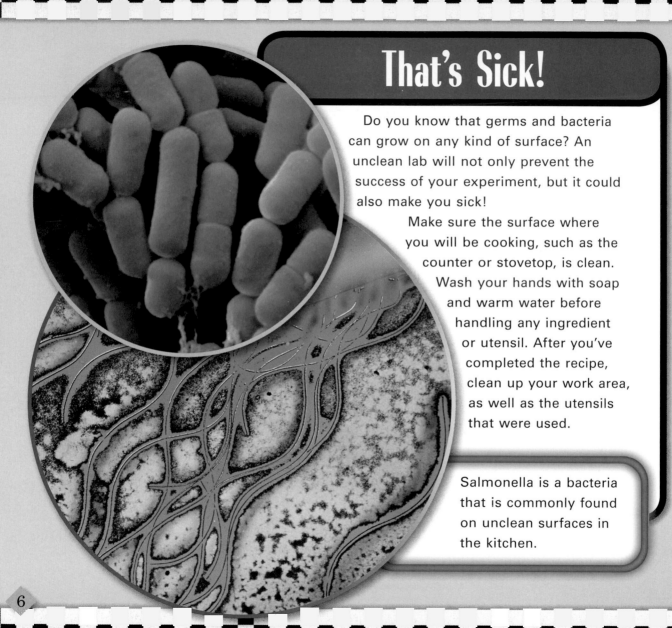

Do you know that germs and bacteria can grow on any kind of surface? An unclean lab will not only prevent the success of your experiment, but it could also make you sick!

Make sure the surface where you will be cooking, such as the counter or stovetop, is clean. Wash your hands with soap and warm water before handling any ingredient or utensil. After you've completed the recipe, clean up your work area, as well as the utensils that were used.

Salmonella is a bacteria that is commonly found on unclean surfaces in the kitchen.

Hot Topic!

Refer to the flow charts below before you begin any recipe. These flow charts will help keep you safe during the experiment.

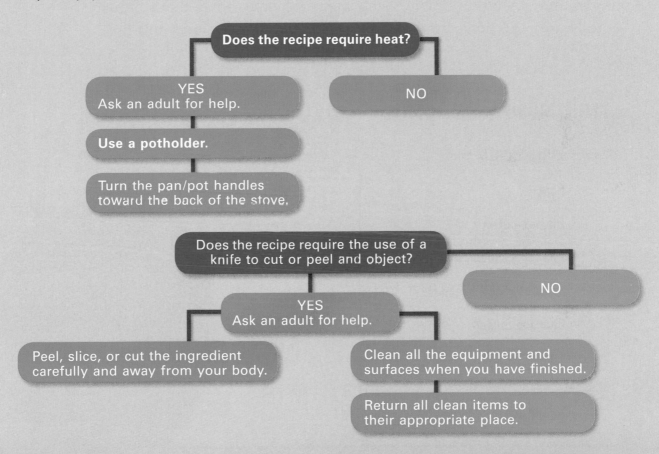

Does the recipe require heat?

YES
Ask an adult for help.

NO

Use a potholder.

Turn the pan/pot handles toward the back of the stove.

Does the recipe require the use of a knife to cut or peel and object?

NO

YES
Ask an adult for help.

Peel, slice, or cut the ingredient carefully and away from your body.

Clean all the equipment and surfaces when you have finished.

Return all clean items to their appropriate place.

Sour Apple

Have you ever noticed that if you slice an apple and leave the pieces out very long they turn brown? Who wants to eat an apple that's brown? There is a way to prevent an apple from turning brown. Check this out!

Fruit Salad with Apples

— Ingredients —

1 apple

1 lemon cut in half

1 can of chopped pineapple

1 can of sliced peaches

1 banana, sliced

1 small jar of
maraschino cherries

1 c. of water

— Utensils —

1 large bowl

4 small bowls

Plastic wrap

— Directions —

1. Ask an adult to cut the lemon in half and the apple into three slices.

2. Put one of the apple slices in a small bowl, and cover it with plastic wrap. Place the bowl in the refrigerator.

3. Put one apple slice in a separate small bowl, and place the bowl on the kitchen counter. Leave the bowl uncovered.

4. Fill another small bowl with one cup of water. Squeeze $\frac{1}{2}$ of the lemon over the bowl and allow the juice to mix with the water. Place the remaining apple slice in the water and lemon juice **solution** and be sure it's completely covered. Then put plastic wrap over the top of the bowl. Leave the apple slice in the solution for one minute. Remove the apple from the solution and place it in a dry bowl.

5. Drain the juice from all of the fruit. Put the chopped pineapple, sliced peaches, banana slices, and maraschino cherries into the large bowl. Stir the ingredients until the fruit is mixed evenly, and cover the bowl with plastic wrap. Place the bowl of mixed fruit in the refrigerator.

6. Wait for approximately 30 minutes, compare the three apple slices.

Something in the Air

You may have noticed that the apple slice that was placed on the counter turned brown very rapidly. This occurred because the apple slice was exposed to the air. Apples, as well as many other types of fruit, experience a chemical reaction when they're exposed to oxygen. This type of chemical change is called **oxidation**.

The apple slice that was refrigerated and covered in plastic wrap didn't turn brown as quickly as the exposed apple slice.

covered in plastic wrap and kept in refrigerator

left on the counter

soaked in lemon and water

The apple slice soaked in water and lemon juice did not turn brown because of the citrus in the lemon juice. Citrus fruits (like lemons) contain a large amount of vitamin C, which slows down the oxidation process. By soaking certain types of fruit in a citrus solution, you can postpone the oxidation process.

After you have completed the experiment, add the apple slices to the large bowl of mixed fruit and enjoy.

What a Lemon!

Recipes for apple pie sometimes call for lemon juice, which is squeezed over the apple slices before the pie is placed in the oven. Why would you squeeze a lemon over the apple slices?

11

It Disappeared!

Next time you are enjoying a cold drink made with water and a powdered fruit mix, remember that you're not only tasting the outcome of an experiment, you're also drinking a solution! A solution is a liquid containing something dissolved in it.

A powdered fruit mix is primarily made out of sugar. It is considered a **solute** because it dissolves when it's mixed with a liquid. Water is a **solvent** because it eventually dissolves the solute. Water will dissolve a solute rapidly when it's shaken or stirred.

Water will dissolve a solute such as a drink mix when it is stirred.

Cool Down

Several factors can affect how quickly a solute will mix with a solvent, including temperature. Cooler temperatures reduce the rate at which a solute dissolves.

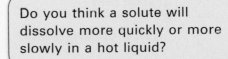

Do you think a solute will dissolve more quickly or more slowly in a hot liquid?

The following recipe will demonstrate how temperature can affect the formation of a solution.

Pink Solution

— Ingredients —

$\frac{1}{2}$ c. of water, hot

$\frac{1}{2}$ c. of water, chilled

$\frac{1}{2}$ c. of water, warm

$\frac{1}{2}$ c. of sugar

Red food coloring

— Utensils —

1 small bowl

3 clear drinking glasses

Wax paper

— Directions —

1. In the small bowl, mix the sugar with three drops of red food coloring.

2. Pour the hot water into one of the clear drinking glasses. Pour the warm water in another drinking glass and the chilled water in the remaining glass.

3. Add 1 tsp. of pink sugar to each glass. Observe for five minutes. Do not shake or stir the glasses!

4. Stir each solution, and observe for two minutes.

Chill Out!

The sugar solute particles in each glass will eventually mix with the water solvent, forming a pink solution. You will notice that the sugar dissolves quickly in the hot water. The water dissolves slower in the glass containing warm water and much slower in the glass containing the chilled water.

Based on the outcome of this experiment, why do you think the directions on the back of different kinds of drink mixes require you to stir the water? Since most powder drink mixes suggest that you use cold water, can you imagine how long it would take to enjoy a glass of your favorite drink mix if you didn't stir the water?

hot water   warm water   chilled water

Using the results from the previous experiment, let's take our recipe one step further and make pink lemonade!

Pink Lemonade

— Ingredients —

Remaining $\frac{1}{2}$ c. of pink sugar (from previous experiment)

1 c. of water, hot

2 c. of water, chilled

2 lemons

Sugar solution (using the solution from all 3 glasses in the previous experiment)

Ice cubes

— Utensils —

1 pitcher

— Directions —

1. Pour the hot water into the pitcher, and stir in the sugar until it dissolves completely .

2. Cut the two lemons in half then squeeze both parts of the lemon over the pitcher.

3. Stir in the pink sugar solution from the previous experiment.

4. Add chilled water.

5. Serve in a glass over ice. Enjoy!

Like Oil and Water

No matter how hard you try, the ingredients in some recipes refuse to stick together. The ingredients in some salad dressings, for example, never completely dissolve and instead form two distinct layers that you can clearly see.

Vinaigrette salad dressings are made by combining oil with vinegar. Although both oil and vinegar are liquids, the oil cannot dissolve the vinegar and the vinegar cannot dissolve the oil. Even if you pour oil and vinegar in the same container and shake the ingredients rapidly, the two liquids never completely dissolve. Liquids such as these, which do not form a solution after they're mixed together, are called **immiscible** liquids.

The following experiment will show the separation of two immiscible liquids.

Oil and Vinegar Mixture

— Ingredients —

1 c. of vegetable oil

6 Tbs. of red wine vinegar

— Utensils —

2 clear jars with lids

— Directions —

1. Pour three tablespoons of vinegar and one-half cup of vegetable oil into each jar. Do not stir the ingredients. You will notice that the oil will rise to the top while the vinegar sinks to the bottom.

2. Place the lids on the jars, and shake one jar rapidly for five seconds. Shake the second jar for 10–15 seconds.

3. After several seconds, compare the size of the oil and vinegar droplets. In which jar do the droplets appear smaller?

You may have noticed that the oil and vinegar in both jars mixed together temporarily. By shaking these ingredients, you were reducing the size of the oil and vinegar particles and enabling the ingredients to mix together, but only for a short time.

The droplets in the jar that was shaken for 15 seconds should have appeared smaller than the droplets in the jar shaken for just a few seconds. The longer you shake the ingredients, the longer it takes for the oil particles as well as the vinegar particles to reunite.

Can you predict what would happen to the size of the droplets if you were to shake a jar for 20 seconds?

The jar on the left was shaken for 15 seconds while the jar on the right was shaken for 5. How would you describe the difference between the contents of each jar?

Fast Food!

Each time you shake a bottle of vinaigrette salad dressing, you're undergoing a scientific experiment! By shaking the oil and vinegar, you're temporarily combining two immiscible liquids.

In order to prevent the oil and vinegar from separating too quickly, however, you must pour the dressing over your salad and eat fairly quickly! But if you add a not-so-secret ingredient to your salad dressing, you may be able to enjoy your meal (and avoid a stomachache caused from eating too fast.)

Let's take our experiment one step further and add mustard to the "mix."

Mustard Mix

— Ingredients —

2 tsp. of mustard (liquid)

— Utensils —

1 jar filled with oil and vinegar (from the previous experiment)

— Directions —

1. Add the mustard to the jar of oil and vinegar.

2. Shake the jar for 15 seconds until the mustard mixes with the oil and vinegar.

When you shake the ingredients together, the mustard particles mix with the oil and vinegar droplets to form an emulsion. An **emulsion** is created when immiscible liquids are mixed together but do not separate. The mustard extends the amount of time it takes for the immiscible liquids to form separate layers. After several minutes, the separate layers will form again.

In the next experiment, we'll use the mustard emulsion to create your very own salad dressing!

Mustard Vinaigrette

— Ingredients —

Oil, vinegar, and mustard emulsion (from the previous experiment)

1 tsp. of salt

$\frac{1}{4}$ tsp. of pepper or paprika

Lettuce, shredded

1 carrot, grated

1 tomato, chopped

1 cucumber, sliced

— Utensils —

1 Large salad bowl

— Directions —

1. Add the salt and pepper (or paprika) to the mustard emulsion from the previous experiment. Mix the ingredients until the dressing appears smooth.

2. Wash and drain the lettuce until it's completely dry, and place it in the bowl.

3. Add the carrots, cucumbers, and tomatoes.

4. Serve the dressing on the side or pour it over your salad.

This Tastes Much "Butter"

Think about the differences between butter and milk. Butter is a thick spread that is made mostly from fat. Milk is a thin liquid that is made mostly of water, vitamins, minerals, and protein. Although these two substances seem very different, butter is actually **derived** from milk through a process that's more scientific than you may think.

Fresh milk that comes from a cow will form a layer of yellow droplets if the milk is not stirred. These tiny droplets that naturally rise to the top layer of fresh milk are called butterfat. Eventually, a small amount of milk will rise to this top layer of butterfat. This mixture of butterfat and milk is called cream. The cream will thicken if it's churned, or mixed, for an extended period of time. This thickened cream is butter.

In the next experiment, you learn how to make butter and buttermilk!

Butter and Buttermilk

— Ingredients —

1 c. of heavy cream or whipping cream

1 clear jar with a lid

— Utensils —

1 measuring cup

Strainer

— Directions —

1. Pour the heavy cream into the jar, and seal the jar with a lid.

2. Shake the jar a few times.

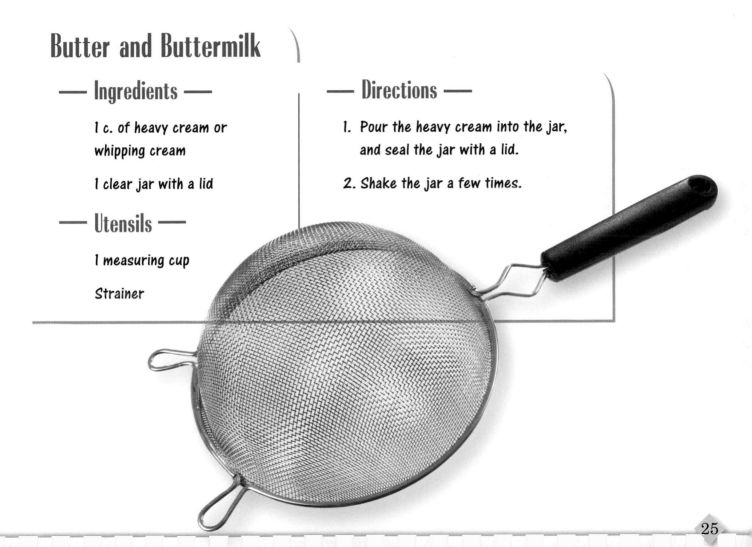

The ingredients inside the jar should begin to resemble whipped cream. Continue shaking the jar until a lump of butter forms inside and mixes with the thick liquid. This combination of milk and butter is called buttermilk.

Using the strainer, drain the excess buttermilk from the butter into the cup. Put the butter back into the jar and place it and the cup in the refrigerator.

Close Encounter

In the last experiment, did you notice that the droplets of butterfat joined together? The droplets began to **coalesce** to form larger droplets of butterfat. Eventually, the butterfat completely separated from the creamy liquid.

Pass the Syrup!

The following recipe will show you how to make delicious buttermilk pancakes using the ingredients from the last experiment.

Buttermilk Pancakes

— Ingredients —

1 c. of all-purpose flour

2 Tbs. of sugar

$\frac{1}{2}$ tsp. of baking soda

$\frac{1}{2}$ tsp. of baking powder

$\frac{1}{2}$ tsp. of salt

1 c. of buttermilk (from the last experiment)

1 egg

2 Tbs. butter (from the last experiment)

Cooking oil

Maple syrup

— Utensils —

2 large bowls

1 frying pan

Spatula

Measuring cup

— Directions —

1. Mix the flour, sugar, baking soda, baking powder, and salt in one of the large bowls.

2. In a separate bowl, mix the buttermilk and egg together.

3. Heat the butter from the last experiment in a microwave until it's melted.

4. Pour the melted butter in the bowl of dry ingredients. Add the buttermilk and egg mixture.

5. Mix all of the ingredients until the pancake batter looks smooth.

6. Put some oil in the frying pan, and heat it on the stove. Ask an adult to help you, because hot oil can spatter. When the cooking oil begins to bubble, fill $\frac{1}{3}$ of the measuring cup with the pancake batter.

7. Pour the batter in the frying pan. You may be able to cook more than one pancake at a time depending on the size of your frying pan.

8. Allow the pancake to cook on one side until tiny bubbles form on top and the bottom appears golden brown. Have the adult use a spatula to flip the pancake, and allow it to cook on the other side for one or two minutes.

9. After the pancakes have finished cooking, serve them with maple syrup.

Not So Fresh, But Fruity

Lots of people love grapes! This plump and juicy fruit is usually eaten by the handfuls. Many people also love raisins even though they stick to your teeth. These two foods seem so different that it's hard to believe they're actually the same fruit!

The process of drying fruit and other foods has been around for centuries. Drying fruit was done in the past to preserve food and prevent exposure to certain kinds of mold and bacteria. Such organisms that grow on food are called **microbes**. These microscopic organisms eventually ruin many types of fresh foods. However, drying food prevents the growth of these microbes.

The following experiment will show you how to dry fruit.

Dried Apples

— Ingredients —

1 apple

— Utensils —

Small bowl
Knife
Baking pan
Cake rack
Food scale (that measures ounces)
Paper
Pencil

— Directions —

1. With the help of an adult, peel and cut the apple into thin slices. Next weigh the apple slices using the scale, and write down the apple's total weight.

2. Place the cake rack on the baking pan, and then place the apples on the cake rack.

3. Heat the oven to 170 degrees. After the oven has reached this temperature, place the apples in the oven. (Ask an adult for help.)

Check the apples every hour over the next three hours. Remove the apples from the oven when they appear leathery, and allow them to cool. Next, weigh the dried apple slices and compare them to their original weight.

You will notice that the dried apple slices weigh less compared to when they were fresh. You may have also noticed that the dried slices appear smaller and thinner. The process of drying the apples removed a large percentage of water from the fruit. Different kinds of mold and bacteria cannot grow on such dry substances, so the dried apples should stay preserved much longer than the fresh apples.

Place the dried apples from the experiment in a bowl of hot water for 30 minutes. You will notice that the apples will regain some moisture. The process of restoring water to the dried fruit is called **reconstitution**.

You will experiment with reconstituting fruit in the next recipe to create a tasty ice cream topping.

Dried Fruit Topping

— Ingredients —

Reconstituted apples
(from the previous experiment)

$\frac{1}{4}$ c. of raisins

$\frac{1}{4}$ c. of dried apricots

$\frac{1}{4}$ c. of dried peaches

2 Tbs. of sugar

2 c. of hot water

Vanilla ice cream

— Utensils —

Large Pot

— Directions —

1. Cut the dried apricots and peaches into small, bite-sized pieces. Place the apricots and peaches in the large pot and add the raisins.

2. Have an adult add the hot water to the large pot, making sure that the fruit is completely covered. Allow the fruit to soak for 20 minutes.

3. Next add the reconstituted apples and the sugar to the pot. Bring the ingredients to a boil.

4. Have an adult reduce the heat of the burner to low, and allow the fruit to simmer for 10–15 minutes or until the fruit is tender.

5. Remove the pot from the heat, and allow the fruit to cool for several minutes. Serve the reconstituted fruit topping over vanilla ice cream.

Protein Power

Foods such as milk, eggs, beans, and meat contain large amounts of **protein**. Proteins are made up of different enzymes and amino acids, which are a necessary part of our diet.

Foods that are rich in protein undergo a process known as **denaturing** when they are cooked.

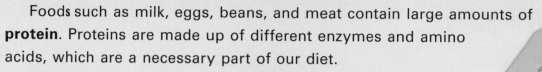

The next experiment will show you how proteins change when they are denatured.

Milk and Vinegar Mixture

— Ingredients —

1 c. of milk

1 Tbs. of vinegar

— Utensils —

1 drinking glass

— Directions —

Pour the vinegar and milk into the glass and stir. Allow the mixture to sit for 15 minutes. Stir the mixture a few more times.

What's different about the mixture? Try stirring it a few more times to see if the mixture returns to a more fluid state.

Substances that are rich in protein (like milk) will thicken when they're exposed to more acidic substances (like vinegar). By mixing the vinegar with the milk, the protein molecules in the milk change shape and clump together. This causes the milk to denature, or thicken. You may have noticed when you tried to stir the mixture a second time that the mixture did not return to its original state.

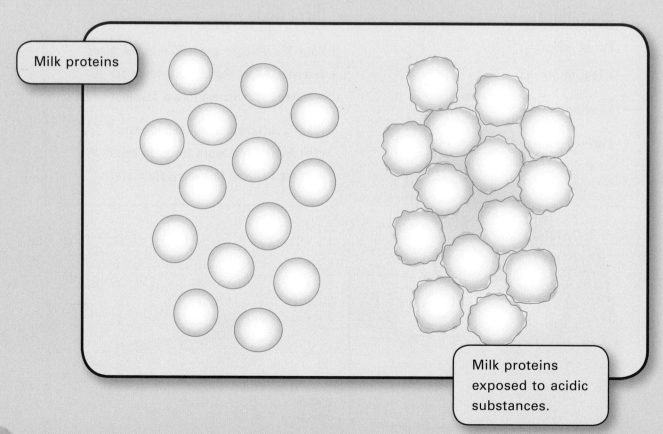

Milk proteins

Milk proteins exposed to acidic substances.

When a special kind of bacteria is added to milk, the sugar that naturally occurs in milk, called **lactose,** is eaten by the bacteria. The added bacteria produces a lactic acid when it comes in contact with lactose. This causes the milk to thicken and taste sour.

The process of converting lactose to lactic acid is called **fermentation**. People have been eating fermented milk products, such as cottage cheese, yogurt, buttermilk, and sour cream, for hundreds of years.

Cottage cheese is loaded with milk proteins. The clumps in cottage cheese are called *curds* while the watery part of cottage cheese is called *whey*.

You'll need the vinegar and milk mixture from the previous experiment in the next recipe to make biscuits.

Biscuits

— Ingredients —

2 c. of flour

2 tsp. of baking powder

$\frac{1}{2}$ tsp. of baking soda

$\frac{1}{4}$ tsp. of salt

4 Tbs. of butter or margarine, chilled

1 c. of sour milk (from the previous experiment)

— Utensils —

2 large bowls

1 baking pan

pastry cutter

spatula

— Directions —

1. Have an adult preheat the oven to 450°F. Mix the flour, baking powder, baking soda, and salt in a large bowl.

2. Cut the butter (or margarine) into small cubes; then mix the butter with the dry ingredients.

3. Use a pastry cutter to evenly mix the butter with the dry ingredients.

4. Add the sour milk from the previous experiment to the butter and dry ingredients. Stir all of the ingredients until the batter appears moist and sticky.

5. Next use a tablespoon to scoop out the batter onto the baking pan. The raw biscuits should be evenly spaced about one inch apart.

6. Bake the biscuits for 10–15 minutes or until they appear golden brown.

"Egg-cellent!"

In the next experiment, you'll discover a way to denature protein using an egg.

Fried Egg

— Ingredients —

1 egg

Cooking oil

— Utensils —

Small bowl

Teaspoon

Small frying pan

Spatula

— Directions —

1. Crack the egg into a small bowl.

2. Tilt the bowl slightly, and watch how the egg slides around. (Observe how slimy the egg white, or clear part of the egg, is.)

3. Pour two or three tablespoons of cooking oil into the frying pan so the egg doesn't stick to the pan. Ask an adult to heat the pan on medium heat. (Make sure that the egg yolk doesn't break as you add the egg to the heated pan. Watch the egg as it cooks.)

4. Cook the egg for approximately five minutes.

5. Next ask an adult to help turn the egg on the other side using the spatula.

6. Continue cooking the egg for one minute.

When the egg is heated, the structure of the protein molecules thicken. As the egg continues cooking, it converts from a liquid to a solid. The yolk begins to harden and turn into a solid form as well.

The process of changing a protein from a liquid to a solid is called **coagulation**.

You will use the fried egg from the previous experiment to make a traditional fried egg sandwich.

Fried Egg Sandwich

— Ingredients —

1 fried egg (from the previous experiment)

1 English muffin

Salt and pepper

1 slice of cheese

Mayonnaise (optional)

— Utensils —

Toaster

— Directions —

1. Split and toast the English muffin.

2. After the muffin is toasted, add cheese and the fried egg from the last experiment.

3. Sprinkle the egg with salt and pepper. Add mayonnaise to your sandwich and enjoy!

Now That's Crumby!

If you look closely at a slice of bread, you will notice hundreds of little holes. These holes are formed by a microbe called yeast. Yeast is a single-celled plant that belongs to the fungi group; and it's the primary ingredient in most breads.

In the following experiment, you will discover how yeast causes bread dough to grow in size.

Yeast Experiment

— Ingredients —

$2\frac{1}{4}$ tsp. of baker's yeast

1 Tbs. of sugar

1 Tbs. of flour

4 c. of warm water

— Utensils —

Candy thermometer

3 clear drinking glasses

3 spoons

Measuring cups

Table/teaspoon

Large pot

— Directions —

1. Ask an adult to slowly heat 3 cups of water in a pot. Use the candy thermometer to check the temperature. The water should be heated to about 105–110°F.

2. Add $\frac{3}{4}$ cup of the warm water to each of the three glasses.

3. Next add equal amounts of baker's yeast to the glasses of warm water, and allow the baker's yeast to dissolve in each glass.

4. Add flour to one of the glasses, and add sugar to the other. Do not add anything else to the third glass.

5. Place all three glasses in the pot, which should still contain more than two cups of warm water in it. The warm water will keep the yeast at the proper temperature. Observe the yeast over the next five minutes.

Up, Up, and Away!

By "feeding" flour or sugar to the yeast in the last experiment, the yeast was able to grow. Unlike other plants, yeast is a fungus that is unable to produce it's own food. Instead, yeast must receive its nourishment from other sources in the environment. (In this case, sugar or flour was added to the yeast's environment.)

The glass that did not include flour or sugar is called a **control**. Scientists often "control" part of an experiment in order to observe changes, which helps **validate** their results.

Bread dough rises when it's heated in an oven because it's exposed to a gas called carbon dioxide. Carbon dioxide traps the air inside the bread, which forces the dough to rise.

FLOUR   SUGAR   CONTROL

You will be able to observe the effects of carbon dioxide trapping air in the next recipe for white bread.

White Bread

— Ingredients —

2 glasses of sugar/flour yeast solution (used in the previous experiment)

4 c. of bread flour

$\frac{1}{2}$ c. of warm water (heated to approximately 105–110°F.)

1 Tbs. of butter, melted

1 tsp. of salt

Utensils

Cooking oil

2 large bowls

Mixing spoon

Loaf pan ($8\frac{1}{2}$" x $4\frac{1}{2}$")

— Directions —

1. Pour the two glasses of yeast mixture into a large bowl.

2. Next add two cups of bread flour, the warm water, the melted butter, and salt. Mix the ingredients using a large spoon for about one minute.

3. Add the additional two cups of bread flour, one cup at a time. Be sure to stir the ingredients after you add each cup of flour.

4. When the dough appears lumpy and no longer sticks to the side of the bowl, it is ready to be kneaded (or pressed).

5. Sprinkle flour on your hands and on the clean surface where you will be kneading the bread. (Bakers put flour on their hands so the dough doesn't stick to their fingers.)

6. Knead (press) the dough for about 10 minutes or until it appears smooth and stretchy.

7. Add two tablespoons of cooking oil to the large bowl. Roll the kneaded dough around inside the bowl, and be sure the dough is completely covered in oil.

8. Cover the bowl with a clean towel, and place the bowl in warm area inside your home for one hour. (The temperature of the room where the bowl is placed should be about 75–80°F.)

9. After the dough doubles in size, punch the dough down a few times with your fist.

10. Smear cooking oil on the inside of the loaf pan, and place the dough inside the pan.

11. Cover the pan with the towel, and place the pan in a warm area (The temperature should remain at 75–80°F) for an additional hour or until the dough doubles in size.

12. Preheat the oven to 450°F.

13. Have an adult put the pan in the oven. Bake the bread at this temperature for ten minutes then reduce the heat to 350°F, and continue baking for 30 minutes.

14. Ask an adult to help you remove the bread from the oven. Allow the bread to cool before serving.

Cooking With Science

Congratulations! You've experimented with science as well as cooking. The best cooks, as well as the best scientists, test their experiments over and over until they're happy with their results. Be sure to practice the recipes in this book until you've mastered the science of cooking.

# Glossary

coagulation the process by which a liquid becomes a soft solid

coalesce to grow or join together

control the factor in an experiment that remains unchanged

denature to change a protein's structure using heat or acid

derived something that comes from another source

emulsion a mixture of two immiscible liquids that do not separate

fermentation a process by which certain substances or organisms break down other substances

immiscible a description given liquids that do not form a solution when mixed together

microbes microscopic organisms

oxidation a chemical reaction that some foods undergo when exposed to oxygen

protein a dietary substance found in animals and plants

reconstitution the restoring of a dried substance to its liquid form by adding water

solute a substance that dissolves in a liquid

solution a liquid mixture containing a dissolved substance

solvent the substance in a solution that dissolves a solute

validate to prove

Index